Riccardo Tomasi

Macrobiotics Revealed

The Health Handbook
I Cured Myself By Eating

Youcanprint Self-Publishing

Title | The Health Handbook. I Cured Myself By Eating - Macrobiotics Revealed.
Author | Riccardo Tomasi
ISBN | 978-88-93060-07-3

Youcanprint Self-Publishing
Via Roma, 73 – 73039 Tricase (LE) – Italy
www.youcanprint.it
info@youcanprint.it
Facebook: facebook.com/youcanprint.it
Twitter: twitter.com/youcanprintit

This book is dedicated to all those who suffer from sickness, to the children of Africa and Asia that still die from terrible diarrhoea, to the homeless, to those oppressed by dictatorships and communism, to the victims of war and to those who have suffered violence, injustice and torture.
It is also dedicated to the memory of my beloved grandparents, Nereo and Amelia and Giorgio and Libera.

Thank you Katya.

INDEX

Change your world, that is your intestinal contents! Learn to consume only two or three foods per meal, to discover their true healing power. My dietary experience led me to these considerations: I was able to identify foods that prevented me from healing, i.e. all dairy products, sausages, rice and certain cooked and raw vegetables. Then, I got the idea that many other people could have similar dietary problems because our bodies are the same and because I had been watching and listening to what other people were eating. The result of my (and others') research is this book, whose title means that it is indeed possible for all to cure themselves by changing diet, introducing certain foods and giving up other everyday foods for a period of at least two or three weeks. Things that harm me, through illnesses that I had, are the same that harm all of you, who, like me, suffer from the same illnesses. But many will say, "It is not like that".

My answer is this: For any disease you have, learn to observe and understand what foods are bad for you, considering my reflections and, if you so wish, using this handbook as a guide for your health. The instinct of the sick is severely flawed and often favours the wrong foods. To make a significant change in your diet, you must be constant, at least for a few weeks or months, in order to develop the right instinct.

Then, if we don't feel great, we can just remember what we ate and change foods, the bread, rice or cereal that we eat the most. In this way, you can learn how to change cereals or give up the cereal (meat, dairy products and vegetables) that you are used to, for an appropriate period of time. Eat only natural unprocessed or little processed foods. **We are sick of too much food: if we eat little and select foods, we can easily heal ourselves in seven to ten days, without medicine!**

When we are sick seeking quick help in a tablet, in a syrup, an injection, is a trap. Changing your diet (preferably preceded by a bit some fasting) requires a little time in order to see benefits, but is a safe therapy that soon leads to great satisfaction. You need just a little patience to stop that suffering. My story is proof of how useless and harmful medicines and medical tests can be and how many lies doctors tell in order to instil fear in their patients to justify themselves as the only possessors of knowledge about disease. Doctors are very careful not to reveal the number of their failures, but I have known them and here will describe them. Furthermore, the results I achieved with natural food are incomparably more significant and satisfactory than many expensive and completely ineffective medical practices, which give minimal results at an extremely high cost in terms of suffering and state funding. Learning to use natural foods as true and proper medicines we can discover that their healing power is much higher than that of drugs. And you can gradually understand what has been harming you all along. This has been my experience. Learn to heal yourself as I did. It's easy. And as for antibiotics, they are very harmful and do not cure any infection, but, in fact, weaken the body. Following I explain how I recovered from very severe infections without antibiotics. It is absolutely not true that antibiotics are necessary. They do a lot damage, first of all to the intestine and teeth (and to all animals in general). And when the damage is done, it is difficult to remedy and efforts to do so are illusory. And like antibiotics are many other medicines, first of all psychiatric drugs, literally poisons.

Psychiatrists, able to contradict anyone, to deny the rights of others by imposing their care are absolutely poisonous too.

The shrink says, "I will take care of you", "So, tell me, how do you feel today?" Whatever you feel, Doc has the right pill. Visions? Smells? Noises? Voices? Or strange thoughts, like, being afraid to go out? Get angry for no apparent reason? Having weird dreams? Depressed? Have contrasting thoughts? Keep thinking about the same things all the time? Have questionable

reasoning? Crying all the time? Getting fat for no reason? Perhaps after taking the pills? Diarrhoea without end? Delusional thoughts? "Then, it's serious". "The judge is getting agitated, he's tough and not to be argued with". "It's an imperative, you have to take the pills".
Then, the doctor who cures crazy thoughts realizes that he needs the pills too... but doesn't take them.
Tchaikovsky got it right, we used to say, Grandpa Nereo and me. The great doctor for whom the street is a room of lights and stars, but, after a few steps along the way of the doctor, life takes over: "No, no, now there's this and that". But you are down, while reality is up and you're sick. You will only now find salvation in God or in your home.
The main foods harmful to the body are meat, milk, yogurt and cereal, all containing far too many chemicals. The most important are fish, very few select vegetables and cereals, without too many chemicals, but not necessarily wholemeal, that is the best and most popular! Important for the mind! Meat while being central in Ohsawa's table of foods, in reality is not, and prevents the removal of acids from the body. However, in third place of his list, three being the perfect number for Orientals, Ohsawa, the father of Macrobiotics put fish. Cereals, wheat in particular, help reasoning and are complementary, but not always necessary. One contraindication: be very careful about cigarette smoke, especially if you eat rice, cabbage or other cooked vegetables.

General rules:
Fasting leads to understanding: "Riccardo, did a fish appear to you?", asked jokingly my grandfather Giorgio, one fine day after five days of fasting when I was about five years old. "Yes", I replied, "I saw a fish". It was a sign that I could start eating again, explained grandpa. I had had for a long time continuous abdominal bloating, a stomach ache for months, with unpleasant stools. I went to stay with my grandparents for six days and my grandfather suggested that I fast. Finally, after five days, my sufferings found relief, something that no food had been able to give me. Years passed because my grandfather lived in Treviso and we saw him rarely. I only had him left as a mentor, after the untimely death of my other grandfather, Nereo.
Nereo had been a genius. He taught me extraordinary things, often taking me to have coffee with him (I drank Coca-Cola), or to read the newspaper or simply out for a walk. We lived in Trieste and I seem to remember that we walked around the centre. Then we moved to the suburbs and life was not as good as before. My grandfather was very strong and with colourful tales loved to explain things that were to others unexplainable. No-one spoke as he did and the charm of his stories was unique. We had our own rules, but we practically absolutely agreed on just about everything and he often showered me with praise! When he passed away it left me absolutely empty. I fasted for five days and also began to feel sick. But somehow I found my path. I got sick once again when I was sixteen with a banal colitis, which was actually debilitating and without any effective cure. I no longer remembered the teachings I had received, after long years without work, immersed in a sea of irresolvable problems. Then around 1997, having built up some strength, I came upon the first treatment for some allergies and then for asthma. From there on it was a road paved with false cures, superstitions and trials lasting long years of oblivion. Today, I believe that health and the happiness that comes from it are simply more con-

sistent earlier in life. Losing them as children, the path becomes very difficult. I retrieved them at least partially, but can say that it will still take a little to reach full satisfaction. To be able to recover completely those gifts of childhood would be the most desirable for all. In my opinion, hundreds of different diseases do not exist, there are only a few, more or less as many as there are organs, because a dietary cure is made up of only a few foods. Diseases of individual organs and mental illnesses always start from the bottom of the intestine, particularly from a chronically dirty rectum. For some there are also diseases of the soul, deriving from various sorrows, and here I would recommend a little cereals, a little tomatoes, which bring joy, and a little dairy products, which give strength.

Healing like peace from war, comes from the bottom.
Nature brings joy in every grain of rice and wheat,
in every leaf and root, in every fish and living animal:
more in buckwheat, potato fries and cabbage!

In 1998, I set to work on "Macrobiotics Revealed", which my intention was to be my first book on Natural Medicines. I had been in love with the most famous and extraordinary texts of Manuel Lezaeta and George Ohsawa, which had achieved some success. However, after a first personal study, I wanted to give my own contribution to Natural Medicine, having then realized that there was a lot of good hidden in Macrobiotics, but also and above all a lot of bad. The ups and downs with psychiatrists, who "treated" me and repeatedly hospitalized me against my will (and in those days very badly indeed), delayed me inexorably from bringing to light the work I had with the aim of divulgating of the Art of Health, according to Nature. And so, today, this work comes to you 14 years late.

When you are cured, I just ask a small thing of you:
tell at least 2 people of your choice, who are very sick, of your path of healing!

If we bring our body to neutrality, if we clean inside our bodies, we heal.

The Yin illnesses.

For George Ohsawa, born Yukikazu Sakurazawa, virtually all diseases were Yin, I think due to the fact that he wanted to pass off the assumption that the human body is totally Yang or neutral, which is certainly without foundation.
According to Ohsawa, basically, whether the body is neutral or Yang, Yin can attack and cause disease. The sick body supports scarce amounts of minerals, which are found especially in grains and vegetables, and looks for centrality or neutrality, if you prefer.
For me, however, the body, all bodies and all natural structures, are like a tree, where the main trunk is Yang, after is neutral, or leaves, and outside is Yin, or flowers and fruits. But you have to be extremely careful, because there are natural products such as saffron which are undoubtedly very Yang.

So Yin illnesses: certainly lung and respiratory diseases and issues with skin, hair, stomach, eyes, ears and extremities.
Yin and Yang: intestines and organs, excluding airways.
Yang: bones, teeth and central and peripheral nervous system.

Consequently, differently from the assumption of Ohsawa that all or most of diseases are Yin, for me they are both Yin and Yang. Acupuncturists, though, no doubt, know the subject better than me. If this explanation is so difficult to comprehend, from a nutritional point of view, then just consider how far medical science is from the truth in categorizing hundreds of diseases. I discussed this with Grandpa Giorgio. Ohsawa (I will not explain everything of Ohsawa, but will briefly summarize to arrive at my point), writing in "The Macrobiotic Diet", a tiny little book, refuted all the main health pseudo-science, closely guarded by witch-doctors, pseudo-scientists, quacks and others. He indicated where to look for health, with what means to achieve it and what undermines it, all in a scheme and in the prose of his famous book of a thousand misunderstandings. Let me explain. Ohsawa gave an extremely strict summary and placed a list of main foods within an acidic and alkaline scheme. This scheme, which was voluntarily improper, helped me to begin to understand some of the mechanisms of Yin and Yang, and then make other deductions. Ohsawa had made fun of all the pseudo-science and popular fantasies born far from the sea, giving to each place in his lists a useful food. To say more is very difficult. But with practice, observation and memory, I realized it was fish that is the main rebuilder of health, and also cabbage, cereals and potatoes. And to confirm these theories, I remembered that the health, and especially mental health and therefore physical health, was greater among people who lived near the sea, just as grandpa Giorgio had long sustained. Instead, in the daily practices and traditions of many peoples, particularly of those who live in extensive plains and in mountainous regions, were hidden ancient traditions, periodic cycles and more, but also superstitions, and actually the most serious and widespread mental and physical diseases: mental confusion, depression, loss of happiness, or rather harmony.

In the table Ohsawa created, fish was placed third, but with only memory and experience did I realize that it represented the concept of centrality, or neutrality, which must be achieved in order to reach a state of well-being, both physical and mental. Instead, meats deny neutrality, because life is a paradox, said Ohsawa. Right above his list of the main meats consumed, he put the list of the main fish (even though all the columns, including fruits, dairy products, meats, fish, vegetables and spices, lacked some important elements). Yang is alkaline in contrast to acidic, which is Yin, and in the middle is neutral. Salt and cooking increase alkalinity. The more we cook, the more food becomes basic, or alkaline. If we cook a fruit it loses acidity and becomes sweet, just like vegetables go from being acidic to alkaline.

Therefore, fish, that live in water, a much colder environment than the surface of the earth, are consequently more Yang than the other animals, and all that which in Ohsawa's main scale is placed below, i.e. meat, dairy products and fruit. Animals of the North are more Yang because they have to face the cold and so more extreme conditions of Yin. Thus they are more smaller and weaker. But men and women of the North tend to be bigger, stronger and physically more powerful than those of the South. Men and animals are therefore counterpoised. The North brings goodness, communion between peoples, the concept of mutual aid and of sociability. And it is here that the most evocative melodies and songs originated. Northerners eat a lot of cooked vegetables, Southerners lots of fruit. Spices are also divided into Yin and Yang, but I confess that I do not know quite how to use them and they have not been useful in my healing, despite the fact Ohsawa attributed to them a similarity to gold, in one of his many mysterious lists. Acidity is determined by acidic foods such as dairy and fatty products, but can be amplified by alkaline excess: both deviate from the path of centrality. Vegetables are neutral while raw, but by cooking descend towards Yang (which in our body is at the bottom, i.e. legs). Oils, in the scale of Ohsawa, which I will shortly present, are lower down and

therefore under Yin, but in my experience I can only recommend olive and sunflower oil, other oils being more dangerous and having a heating effect.
To quickly achieve neutrality, which, as I have said, is difficult with the common mentality that says meats and even dairy products are harmless, in my experience, it is best to stay away from them. Naturally, the sick should note that, if their illnesses are Yin, Yang and neutral, caused by excess acids, bases and neutrality (although I will not speak here of those of neutrality), their healing is to be found in the neutral, i.e. fish, cooked cabbage, potatoes and cereals, and sometimes fruit. But healing by fruit, I repeat, is very difficult. Therefore, to rapid achieve neutrality, simply abandon meat and dairy products (sugars are for me almost harmless, even helping the depressed and afraid).

Here is the first scale of Ohsawa:

Fruit, dairy products, meat, fish, vegetables and cereals.
Maximum Yin fruit, neutral centre fish, maximum Yang cereals.

However, on the page of this table of his famous book, meat appeared in the centre.
It starts from the acidic, passing through neutrality or centrality to arrive at the alkaline. In chemistry it is the same: pH-0 is acidic, pH-6 is neutral and pH-14 is alkaline.
This is the origin of the understanding of healing: the terms Yin and Yang indicate nothing but acidity and alkalinity. According to Master Ohsawa, if the body suffers from one of the two excesses, it is enough to FIND THE APPROPRIATE FOOD (consuming it for several days) in order to return to the centre. The cure was so simple that Ohsawa was amazed to learn that no-one in the West understood it and this is why he filled his books with irony and veiled anger. He had also been a witness to the two atomic bombs that annihilated Hiroshima and Nagasaki, and his brothers, sisters and mother died of tuberculosis treated with antibiotics. In a false world, he exported his magic cure: eat only rice for ten days.

Taking as a reference point the centrality of the human body made of flesh, the word "meat" in the table of Ohsawa was placed precisely in the centre, but wrongly, because meat as food, I realized with experience, deviates from the centre.

Oils, fruit, dairy products, meat, fish, vegetables and cereals.

Fruit is more acidic than dairy products, which also contain a lot of fat and protein, and should be used with caution for the myriad different problems that it carries. After weaning, all animals move away from their mothers to feeding in harmony with nature, from what can easily be collected. We all eat plenty of meat and vegetables (raw and cooked vegetables are very good for the development of intelligence), but keep in mind that cooked vegetables such as potatoes and cabbage, aubergine (or eggplant) and soups are very good for us, but in opposition to what Ohsawa claimed.
Therefore, a simple diet of the following should be right for you:
Pasta and fish
Potatoes and pasta
Pasta and spinach
Cabbage with pasta (and fish) (and fruit)
Potatoes and fish
Aubergine and pasta
Aubergine with fish
Avoid all dairy products, meat and other vegetables

Salads are very helpful for veins, heart and bones. With bread or pasta and tuna, they facilitate weight loss.
Fruit helps the mind, also with paranoia, as it lightens the spirit.

Yin diseases regard mainly respiratory pathways, skin and stomach.
Yang diseases being among the most difficult to heal, the foods here above are among the major factors of cure for virtually all ills (below, in talking about various other diseases, you will find what were my first convictions). I do not have the gift of abso-

lute truth, but all my work can act as a guide for your own personal journey.

And maybe, together, we can construct a whole new way. Have faith and you will soon be smiling!

However, with all these wonderful considerations, I must warn you that your first reaction to any dietary issue should be to stop and think.

If we observe children when they make a mistake with what they are eating, they use temporary abstinence from food to find a solution: they are looking for the right food! "Why don't I feel good today?" Children stop and think, and they are right to do so! Children slowly learn about food and the effects that it has on them. When they make mistakes (if adults do not force them to eat), children want to stop, fast, skip a few meals, because they know that they do not feel well. They want to understand what made them feel bad and want to recover their lost happiness. "Today is not like yesterday: what happened to me?" They want to find a solution and being very smart, much more so than their parents, they look for a concentration or nothingness. But how many mothers do not know how to eat well? Children make mistakes because they are learning, but they have to make mistakes! Then they try out different tricks, rules, or ask Jesus to restore their personal Paradise Lost. Children seek out what has harmed them and are afraid to just go on. They need a few hours or days to find the courage to return to food, naturally, if they can easily find on their table what they need to feel better, or otherwise nothing, peace will soon return anyway. But if this does not happen, the children, despite their trial and error, can fall into problems and will suffer the harmful consequences, like everyone else. Fasting is also a cure for both children and adults. But everyone is looking for healing through food, often driven, unfortunately, by a deviated instinct. Many have suggested fasting as a cure, but each person must find and learn for himself. That is why we can say: be your own doctor and no-one can take responsibility for your healing, but yourself. And I myself was once adrift in the stormy ocean of even natural remedies and medicines.

For over twenty, or thereabouts, I have carefully studied the texts of George Ohsawa, the father of Macrobiotics. Endlessly reading and rereading his poetry in prose and many occult messages, I looked for the true meaning of his words. I was sure that hidden between the lines of the handwritten pages of this incredible Master, with every word and every food carefully placed, there was something secret to discover, which had remained inaccessible for me for many long years. I eventually got to the bottom of this secret, I believe, and here I am retransmitting it to you, for your and our common good.

Mother Nature is like an orchestra playing the most wonderful music. When Ohsawa wrote 'rice', he meant something else, perhaps fruit (or fish, which was third of his listings). Indeed, the word 'apple' was placed last in the column of fruit on the right. It was last and not there by chance, but instead 'rice' was the first word in the cereals column.

"What does this have to do with anything?!", I hear you say.

The apples were in the place of lemons, which being the most acidic of fruits, in that scale (an acid-alkaline scale), should have been at the bottom. **Apples, fruit and fish can be eaten alone, rice NO**.

The scales of Ohsawa.

Foods:
Cereals, vegetables, fish, meats, dairy products, fruit, oils, beverages, spices to complete.
Fruit:
Pineapples, papaya, mangoes, grapefruit, oranges, bananas, figs, **lemons**, pears, grapes, peaches, melons, plums, almonds, peanuts, cashew nuts, watermelon, cherries, hazelnuts, green olives, black olives, strawberries, blackberries, chestnuts, **apples**.

Obviously there were also scales for all the cereals, vegetables, meats and so on.

Foods are thus in order from alkaline to acidic, until we get to fruit.

In Ohsawa's scales, then, lemons are not in last place, which instead is given over to apples. It did not add up. Lemon is without a doubt the most acidic fruit. Why such a simple mistake? Could such an intelligent man as Ohsawa be wrong? No. This means that this exchange of places must have been therefore been intentional, one of many traps set.
It is with messages like this that Ohsawa filled his books, accompanied by so much irony.

Apples placed there:
1) Being at the bottom, it could mean that they are meant for animals (in the Bible the apple was given to Eve by the serpent, and also corn is at the end of the left column of cereals).
2) Lemons instead of apples in the central position were clearly out of place.
3) Lemons are fine with fish if the body is not too acidic and also with sugars.
4) You cannot only eat cereals for days and days, because it is harmful.
5) Rice with dairy products are harmful to thought and teeth.

So even here Ohsawa, a man born on an island, albeit the huge island of Japan, needs to be understood and carefully studied!

Vinegar and honey. George Ohsawa, our great friend and teacher, in addition to being a sublime writer, gave the world one of his powerful medicines for all those who suffer from the ills of Yang. Ohsawa was joking when he said that this remedy was valid for only a small number of very Yang people. In the West, we are all very much Yin or very much Yang, i.e. extremists! (Ohsawa even did the math, enumerating by categories of illness the sick of Yin and Yang). Indeed, we eat a lot of meat (that lead us towards the perversity of Yang) and many dairy products (animals are the opposite of man, eating a lot of Yang and neutral, with only monkeys eating a lot of fruit). Vinegar and honey, which is Yin + Yang (acidic + sweet), is also a good remedy for toothache, which is Yang (too many dairy products and rice). Toothache is caused by a contraction of nerves, which are shortened, and is favoured by rice and dairy products. It is cured by eating (a little) fish, wheat, buckwheat, aubergine (eggplant) and potatoes. Ohsawa wrote that the cinders of roasted aubergine could be used to cure toothache! Have you ever tried eating aubergine with a little pasta when you have toothache? Try it, and for several days! Do you realize that not even a hundred years ago there were very few dentists with even crazier equipment than today? But what else could heal people in the past if not fasting and diet? Before writing these lines, I personally tested vinegar and honey, even with very little water. It is a great remedy for the ills of Yang, **but not for asthmatics, which are Yin**.

Church in the Ukraine among the clouds: thank you Lord.

Colitis and chronic diarrhoea are two of the most difficult illness to cure, in my opinion. Imagine a tube within which we have undigested food, faeces, bacteria and water, all at about 37°C, with no air!

What medicine can disinfect this content and simultaneously alleviate inflammation in the organ, the tube that contains it all?

What herbal tea can do this? Only chamomile, I recently discovered, has a strong ability to help, but it must be accompanied with the right foods).

What homeopathic product, chemical or natural?

What miracle can change the bacterial load, which is revitalized and grows whenever the sick eats foods that are nutritious for these bacteria?

Allergies, however, are among the diseases easiest to heal, with the correct nutrition: just stop eating meat (especially sausages) and all dairy products, for at least 2-3 weeks.

Pearls of Ohsawa's Wisdom

George Ohsawa had understood the mechanisms of recovery from bacterial diseases (for example, in "Natural Cures for Incurable Disease", publisher Pratika MEB) and viral diseases through food, but hid his knowledge between the lines of his writings and teased the Western man terrified by these microscopic monsters! He was the first man to define Western doctors as scammers, having seeing his mother, sisters and brother die of tuberculosis, treated unsuccessfully with antibiotics. He saved himself by fasting for sixty days! And then he created the Macrobiotic diet with the Japanese mentality which dictates that the teacher should encourage students, but not give them all the answers! Otherwise, they do not learn!

"Everyone has to learn everything from everyone day and night, especially from a strong and cruel enemy; without a fight you become lazy, weak and stupid. This guide for your life is more than enough in this great school. I have never written a book that responds to so many problems, although I have written more than three hundred in Japanese. In the Orient, the teacher asks questions, but does not give answers, so he fortifies the

judgment of his students. In the great school of happiness and freedom, the only teaching is practice. Theory is merely a product of thought" (from "The Macrobiotic Diet", Astrolabio Editions).
So wrote and argued the Master. And he did not give the answers. He only indicated the way, hidden between the lines of his writings, repeating all the time that life, every phenomenon, is always made up of at least two elements, though in his diet for healing every disease he advised eating only rice for ten days. At least one element was missing!
"My hand trembles, today, and my eyes have been full of tears for many days, but finally in me grew wider knowledge of the Truth. After exactly 35 years from the date of his death, now it is up to me the incredible burden of giving the world the truth about Macrobiotics, of the text that Mr. Ohsawa said would give everyone the possibility of healing oneself perfectly from every disease. The reality, however, was that Nyoiti Sakurazawa voluntarily confused the concepts of Yin and Yang..." - so I started my first book "Macrobiotics Revealed", 1998. But I was stopped by psychiatrists and had to find the evidence and cures for the most difficult of ills, in my experience and knowledge. I was ready to pull apart the teachings of the Master, but inside me I was not alright with it, for the simple reason that the lists created by him followed a very precise order and were not created haphazardly. Today, I have finally received the proof of the goodness and wisdom of George Ohsawa. In 1966, in Tokyo, the world lost its most illustrious teacher.
Unlike our friends outside Europe, we civilized and rich do not have in our colder lands insects or parasites that attack us every day. But we create our enemies within our own bodies, eating too much and the wrong foods, or eating the same things, in the day and for weeks, months, or eating products containing chemicals of which we know nothing, food that is not good and a lot less digestible (just go to poorer countries to notice the difference). We put into our intestines foods that we cannot get rid of properly, which are not like natural foods, free of chemicals, that slip out of the body without damaging it. Our foods harm the body and mind, in a silent but continuous way. Instead of

synoptic, they make us become analytical, rather than simple, they make us cunning, highly intelligent, but totally sceptical, devoid of social feeling, focused only on own personal and unique gain. Disease pollutes the mind first, then the body and life. Without Goodness there is no Justice, because the capacity to fully understand is not there. Changing your diet will allow you, in a short time, to retrieve your best faculties and the desire to do things and laugh!

Here I would like to remember the poor and abandoned in all the world. It gave me great sadness to see, in Brazil, people homeless and jobless, without water or electricity, dressed in rags, wandering in fields without trees, women, men, children, fenced in by tens or hundreds of kilometres of wire netting or immoral barbed wire. In the television programme of the world-travelling chef Fred Chesneau, I saw that Australian Aborigines are relegated to living in the desert with nothing, forced to feed on giant lizards, with very little else, children, the elderly, life-less and hopeless, while just a few miles away beer is drunk cheerfully in one of the most attractive cities of the world. It does not seem that the world lacks money. I appeal to all those who can: I beg you, do something. The world is big, there is an economic crisis in the West: why not give life to an Economic Revolution? The commitment of men and means could lead to acceptable living conditions in the poor world, not only water and industries of exploitation, but a large-scale investment in order to save lives and bring healing plants, housing and work to those who suffer the most. Do you not think that, in a few years, there would be an exceptional return? Those that according to some do not want to work for me are actually sick! Those that live by charity and begging have tough and ugly lives, never have fun and are in perpetual anxiety! Of course they would like to work, as everyone! We have homes, clean clothes, but is it so hard to imagine that others just cannot do it?! Do states only have to spend on hospitals, healthcare, weapons, pollution, roads, lighting and schools? What other services do they give to the citizens of the world? Really, do you have fun in exclusive clubs, with rigid labels? In a padded life?

Who made us like this? Try and guess. Who put cotton wool in the ears of the world? These are two very important questions to think about. And then (it's no joke), are you really deeply religious? For me, true faith comes from recognizing the hand of God in the curative power of food, the most common means at our disposal!

Ohsawa, Revelation & My Vision

Ohsawa in one of his books referred to the seven degrees of Judgment. And he spoke of the qualities of early Christians in not responding to persecution and wickedness. The Book of Revelation of the Bible is addressed to the seven churches of Asia Minor: Ephesus, Smyrna, Pergamum, Thyatira, Sardis, Philadelphia and Laodicea. The faithful were encouraged to resist persecution by the Roman authorities with the promise of the Kingdom. The book talks about persecution by public officials of martyrs of the faith. This persecution constituted a serious danger to the whole of Christianity. It speaks of the opening of the seven seals, the sending of plagues and the Four Horsemen of the Apocalypse (famine, war, pestilence and death). In the second chapter there are seven signs, including the vision of the woman with the child who suffers persecution from the dragon with seven heads and ten horns. The following chapters describe other signs: the beast of the sea, the beast of the earth, the lamb and the virgin, the three angels, the son of man and the angels of the seven plagues. Following the appearance of seven goblets is the announcement of the fall of Babylon and its famous whore. The events include two eschatological battles, separated by a thousand years, the destruction of the empire of the Antichrist with all his followers and Satan chained and helpless. In the intervening thousand years, there is the Kingdom of Christ and martyrs. At the end of time, there is the second and last battle with Satan and he is cast off into the lake of fire, along with death and hell. What remains is the Heavenly Jerusalem. The language of the Apocalypse is characteristically full of visions, images and symbols. It is a futuristic or an eschatological vision, the announcement of the end of the world. It is a historical vision, narrating facts from the 1st century to the second coming of Christ. The book ends with the defeat of the wild beast, the reign of a thousand years, and the Heavenly Jerusalem (source Wikipedia). I wonder: was it not true that in ancient times religions were closely connected with nutrition? And that in food the religious man saw clearly the work of God the Creator, addressed to all that is good? To what judgment might the seven churches of the seven cities of the Apocalypse correspond?

As a child, in Trieste, Italy, at the age of about three years, I began to have visions not in reality, of the living world. They opened like a screen before my eyes, visible only to my brain, with a perfect picture! The first time I was playing while sitting on the green linoleum floor of the dining room of my maternal grandparents in Barcola Trieste, in front of the sea. A wooden curtain opened before my eyes, with steps and dark red curtains on the sides. I was in front, above, watching. Naked men, with horns and tails, entered one by one, moving from left to right and out. The scene closed and I returned to my games. The next day and the following two days, the vision returned, with the same men passing by and I watched. The fourth day was the only time I heard words. I was myself and I was reading through the pages of the Great Book of Life, inflicting penalties on devils for their misdeeds. I forgot all about this, until just years ago. But then, not long after the first four days, I began to see like a TV in my head nice cartoons, funny characters and captions that ran along the bottom. The scene did not bother me and I could get on with other things at the same time. I saw these things for about two or three minutes, every day of my life until the age of about twenty-one. The last caption read, "Free from guilt".

The wrong dietary habits of the sick.

1) Milk, yoghurt, all dairy products, too many vegetables, except for a certain select few, cereals such as rice, puffed cereals and too many chemicals, too much meat and sausages, coffee.
2) Forever eating the same things and only those.
3) Too much industrial, packaged and processed foods.

In Italy, from about 1973, began an economic boom that led to the destruction of the landscape due to the construction of numerous roads and buildings, with the destruction of large green areas and trees. In some cities, they are so obsessed that they cut down trees every year! Trees! With charm in their stature, trees make us look up to the sky, provide shade in the summer, whisper to the wind, clean and perfume the air and colourfully paint the streets in Autumn!
This negatively affects the quality of life for everyone, because cities and countries without large numbers of trees are barren deserts, where man is lost and the quality of life is extremely low. With supermarkets came great displays of packaged and canned products, which by attracting the attention of consumers and housewives at the expense of fresh produce raised proportionally the spread of disease. A society of wellness became in the following years a society of the sick.
Small food stalls disappeared from the streets and with small commercial activities on sidewalks went many traditions. Then came the monsters of construction and new roads. Excessive use of chemistry, first in agriculture and then in the food industry, brought a remarkable loss of Taste and Health. Those responsible are, as usual, politicians and medical facilities and pharmaceutical science at the highest levels, those who give the orders! And those that establish protocols, according to which doctors are required to give the drugs to everyone. Today's generations, frail, thin, with small bones and weak physical structures are the most dramatic sign. Then there are the elderly liv-

ing beyond ninety, weak and sad, lifeless, with no smiles or laughter or hopes, in solitude, attached to expensive drugs and their thousand side effects. Better a bit of good wine or something else, for example, salo, a great Ukrainian lard, and natural foods to happily leave the world at an average of seventy years! A society that glorifies Nature is a happy society, rich in physically strong, spontaneous, funny, intelligent and artistic people. Inhabitants of the twenty-first century, what have we become? We have to fight to claim back our rights, happiness and our natural environment, including nutrition!

4) Eating too much (especially bread, cereals and meat) and too often.

5) Not eating cereals for a long time (which are essential and protective, especially when you intake animal proteins).

6) Inability to change your diet (the diets of the sick are like drugs creating addictions and fear of change).

Genuine food culture, barely surviving in the countryside, is almost extinct elsewhere, where housewives have adapted to not making an effort, content with the ready-made. A healthy man can change his habits at any time, because bad habits he does not have! Healthy men (and women) are intelligent and, in proportion, cheerful and friendly!

7) Eating too late and overeating at breakfast. Germans traditionally eat at 6pm because eating at night can lead quickly to obesity).

8) Breathe. Yes, for those who live in the city, just get in your car and drive out to a lake. When you step down from your car you will immediately breathe a different air!

For some, the first signs of illness is given to them by the mind. Without realizing it, the person intoxicated by the wrong food begins to reason absurdly and incorrectly, says wrong or stupid things, is convinced of being right (and I am not talking about severe mental illness here). And far be it from me to want to offend anyone! The person fails to address problems external to him, focusing only on his own problems. He is not interested in anything beyond himself, because he is constantly in search of what makes him feel bad, even unconsciously. He may have a thousand fears and bad moods! If no-one is there to help, he can go on for months or years before the disorders of the disease clearly manifest themselves. And help might even come from you too. Therefore, the first alarm bell is the mind, which can reflect the state of intoxication of the body in thoughts, words, feelings and behaviours. If the person can immediately correct their diet, they will see immediate improvements and satisfaction in both the mental and physical realms and can avoid disease! And unhappiness.

My Experience: my illness and the medicines I took

I was born in 1963 and so, today, I am fifty-one years old. When I was six I had allergies to dust mites, pollen, grasses from June to July, wool, plaster mould and cat dander.
To "cure" these allergies I was forced to take steroids, antihistamines and dexchlorpheniramine in large doses until the age of thirty-five, almost every day and almost every month of the year, for twenty-nine years! And they call this a "cure"! I was advised to receive vaccinations that would gradually reduce my allergies. Thus I had vaccinations from six until almost eighteen years old to no avail! Allergies and allergic rhinitis means sneezing for hours, swollen eyes, a stuffy and runny nose, inflammation continuing for months and strong even at night. The allergies and rhinitis stopped, apart from asthma, when in 1999 I

decided to no longer eat any kind of dairy products! I then just had asthma for only one or two months a year for a few years. I finally cured my asthma by eliminating also sausages, bread, beer and leavened foods definitively from my diet. I was therefore asthmatic from about ten years old until 2001, twenty-eight odd years! I had to use bronchodilator sprays and constantly check I had them with me, just in case, for years and years. During periods when the asthma attacks were stronger and more frequent, I often spent sleepless nights with the fear of that fateful moment arriving. And it was arriving. Asthma means no longer being able to breathe air, suddenly. Then, I developed colitis at sixteen. I was initially constipated, with mucus, air, very painful spasms, troublesome defecation and exhaustion, every day until around 1998. The "cure" of doctors was lactic enzymes, which gave me diarrhoea rather than relief, and drugs for "intestinal motility", which procured states of exhaustion, palpitations, mental ill-health and a few years of visits to specialists and luminaries, until I decided not to take them anymore and make do by myself.

Because of one drug, Zi*******xa, the colitis became constipation and diarrhoea lasting thirteen endless years, with the most excruciating pain and exhaustion. The other drugs (the most famous and commonly sold) temporarily interrupted the phenomena, which then inevitably began again. These drugs also have an antibiotic effect and their use for a long time is strongly discouraged! Around twenty-four years old I had urethritis. I was "treated" with antibiotics, about a hundred injections and tablets for more than eight months. I had pain from the antibiotics and pain from the infection to no avail. I had diarrhoea, gastritis and some even told me I had become green! Then, I remember, I had otitis already at the age of eighteen. For this too, I took oral and local antibiotics to no avail! Also completely unnecessary were flushes of thermal water up my nose, delivered via a curved iron tube to the ear canal. It was truly painful. Gastritis gave me a few problems, but I was strong and did not go to the doctor. After much trial and error, I began to eat boiled fish with vegetables and a little cereal. I recovered quickly without the aid of anything else and now when I have a little acidity, I just eat some fish and think no more about it! I also had herpes for a year, chronic conjunctivitis, recurring tooth-ache, a serious mental disorder, obesity from pharmaceutical treatments, two infections contracted abroad and myopia! And swelling in my limbs. But I managed to solve all these problems with fasting and eating the appropriate foods! That are simply those that I mentioned above. It is almost all documented and I still have a photocopy of my old driving licence that stated the obligation to wear glasses.

Do medicines really cure?

I distinguish between two types of sick people.
There are the occasionally sick, always healthy, except for momentary ailments, a cold, a headache, a bit of stomach acid or indigestion. They take medicine, swear that it cured them and will not listen to other opinions.
Then there are the chronically sick, which have a sensitivity that the occasionally sick do not have. Only the chronically sick take medicines for years and know that do not cure but are only a temporary remedy, if they do not do serious damage such as silent ulcers in the stomach and oesophagus caused by anti-inflammatory and other drugs of which not even doctors know the real effects. I personally could see what was happening to my mother, with several ulcers and an oesophagus so tight that for months she could no longer eat solids and vomited every day. Did this all happen by chance, or did the drugs she was taking (she was not taking anti-inflammatory drugs but many others) have something to do with it? Fortunately, today my mother is better. I am sure that no-one can end up in these kind of states by just eating normally as did my mother, but the doctors deny any hand in her illness.
The chronically sick pay attention. If they eat only two or three foods per meal, they will realize what is positive for them and what is absolutely not. The occasionally sick are so strong that for them all foods are fine and there are no differences, no

harm. So the chronically sick, thanks to their enhanced sensitivity, perceive and understand the reality, which the occasionally sick do not see!

Which foods proved to be curative effective natural medicine?

Cooked cabbage stopped my thirteen years of diarrhoea, accompanying my normal diet! **Boiled fish** cured me of gastritis in a few days and, when I had cystitis, immediately relieved me of very painful symptoms. Well-cooked perch, canned tuna, cod, hake and squid work well for diarrhoea and the colon. **Buckwheat**, boiled for about fifteen minutes, was another solution to mitigate the violence of diarrheal discharges. From these three foods I received incontrovertible proof so important as to convince me to talk about it publicly.

If you have toothache and neuralgia, eating a lot of cereals, ice cream, vinegar and saffron leads to screaming out in pain! Eat only fish with cooked cabbage, aubergine or buckwheat (or pasta) to breathe a sigh of relief! It makes a big difference!

The most negative trial results I got were with asthma. Compared with all the other ills I suffered, finding the right and wrong nutrition for asthma was by far the most difficult. As ex-asthmatic, I can suggest first of all avoiding all dairy products and eating too much meat. But also avoid leavened foods, beer, mushrooms, canned and processed foods in general, salami, sausages and too much bread! Many people have a naturally healthy diet. They eat a first course of perhaps pasta, a second course of meat or fish, a little vegetables, water or a little wine and fruit between mealtimes. But does this good diet heal both the chronically and occasionally sick? For me, the occasionally sick yes, but the chronically sick meet some resistance to healing and have to resort to making some specific choices in their diet, and with very meagre quantities. The sooner they do so, the sooner they will be smiling once again. It is not possible to heal if between meals you have snacks, sweets, ice-cream, coffee, cigarettes, yoghurt, cheese, canned and processed foods and so on. I have observed that many illness require a very strict regime, such as gastritis, which does not tolerate dairy products, or chronic diarrhoea, which I could only cure after eating a few select foods for more than two weeks! Many vegetables are contraindicated. So is milk, coffee, many fruits and too much food! Chronic illnesses require a change in diet for quite long periods, but do not despair and keep trying. The chronically sick have to gradually learn to choose which foods are suitable for them and which are not. If they continue only with foods positive for them, they can achieve healing and for this reason I give food an enormous importance, that of Natural Medicine. The more severe the disease, the more you have to narrow down the appropriate foods, alternating them and fasting when necessary!

A Slight Hitch: I was eating too much cooked cabbage

About fifty days ago, I had very swollen ankles. I was still smoking and I am sure that I still had inside me the psychoactive drugs I had taken the previous year, in June 2013. These drugs had made me retain fluid, swell and even compromised the health of my teeth, which had started to move around with gums full of blood so as to lead me to avoid using a toothbrush for months. For many days I did not know what to do. I often ate cabbage, bread or pasta, fruit, but the swelling did not go down. I had made the mistake of becoming a vegetarian and was not eating fish. I went on with this serious problem until very recently. I finally relieved the swelling in my ankles and legs with the diet I have spoken about above: fish and pasta, tuna and bread. Following are two photos: the first are my legs on 29th April 2014 and the second are my legs on 7th May!

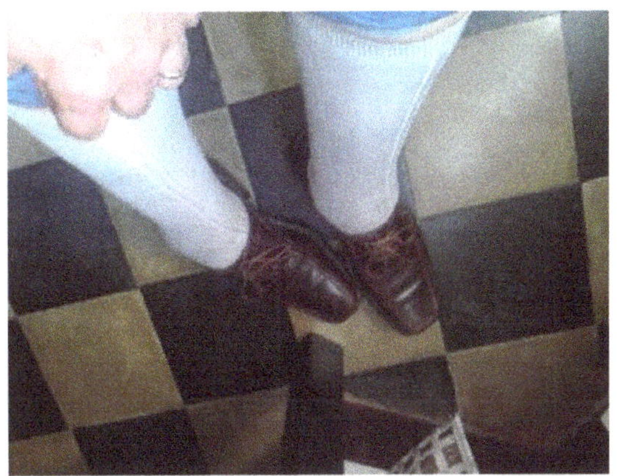

I had been swollen like this for more than thirty days! What would a doctor have said? He would have given me antibiotics and ointments!
The situation on 7th May, having not eaten or drunk that day, simply because I realized that this is the fastest way to solve this problem. The results are clearly evident!

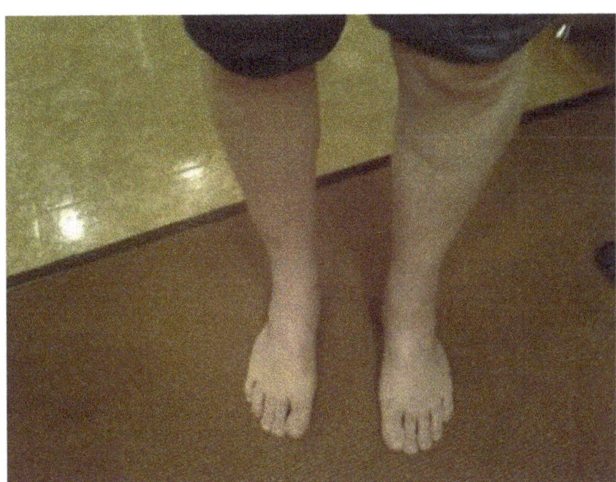

The diet proposed here is not a medicine, in the sense that you may continue to suffer some ills for a few days at the start of

your dietary change or period of semi-fasting. This is because the healing does not happen gradually by degrees but rather suddenly and all at once, after days of perseverance! With colitis, first the unpleasant discharges decrease, then the air and mucus, but you may still suffer right up to the big day of total remission. I do not believe that to heal you must necessarily go through a painful process of expulsion of toxins, as happens in fasting with water alone, where the sick person may even vomit frequently. For me healing means bringing the body back to normality, by taking advantage of the special organs inside us that can opportunely expulse toxins and all that we no longer need, first via the intestine and then the urinary tract!
Semi-fasting works for us in this wonderful way!
The Number 1 health issue is to change our physical landscape, that is change pH and the acidity of the intestine, which is the result of what we eat.

Poor Animals

For sceptics and those of you who no longer believe in anything, try this test: break a chilli-pepper with your fingers and then touch your eye and your tongue. Burns doesn't it? But wait, don't be afraid, now I'll give you the remedy. You don't need to drink water, eat bread or rinse yourself. Just put a bit of oil (any cooking oil) on your fingers, on your burning eyelid and on your tongue. The burning will stop all of a sudden.
I am just a humble observer who has always been in love with Nature and people that are full of life but honest, as so many in Trieste, Friuli, Tuscany, Veneto, Emilia Romagna, Liguria, in the South and the North and everywhere in the world! These people struggle every day against wickedness and dishonesty. They always look for the good and try to correct the deaf and blind! *They have always struggled and cannot stand the evils of this world.* For days I have been eating natural foods as a guest of the dear relatives of my Katya in Ukraine. Here agriculture and farms are still as before, without chemicals (elsewhere made legal by who knows?)!

In Italy, there are animals suffering in stalls, in cages, in shameful chains! Animals are stuffed with antibiotics and hormones to fatten them quickly and earn more money. Chemistry in their fatty tissues becomes something disgusting on the palate. Animals are treated as objects, by ignorant and bad people. Animals are numbed with drugs, real poisons. They are unhappy and scream their suffering in silence to the complete indifference of civil and educated man. They fall ill from processed food and their masters who have completely forgotten what nature is. Animals are locked in cages, aquariums or boxes as objects for fun and companionship, by brainless people. Good and kind animals are forced to become aggressive and dangerous for the satisfaction of their masters, cowards, who do not know how to defend themselves on their own. Animals are fair game for vivisection, practiced by criminal scum. Poor Italy, martyred by unscrupulous and unintelligent people for purely for personal gain. They have made the pig a heavy food, indigestible and also bad for you. And beef, which shrinks in the pan. Vegetables and acidic fruit, which are dangerous to health. They produce salads without any aroma (can you not remember how it was years ago?) and ice-creams that all taste the same. In the past ice-cream parlours were highly sought after for their distinctive flavours. Today, due to the impositions of health authorities, the food products used are to sterilized to a maximum and all ice-cream tastes the same, even though I no longer eat it. Sweets are terribly harmful to those who are suffering from colitis. Eggs are almost indigestible and are incomparable with those of the farm. Bread is to be avoided by all asthmatics. It is all harmful, with excessive and harmful chemicals! Who wanted all this? Who suggested it? Who voted it into legality?

The healthy man feels hunger and thirst every day, the chronically ill almost never! What does this mean? That when heal we will begin to feel hunger and thirst again and many other wonderful but lost sensations that fasting can help us quickly recover.

Time begins to pass ever more quickly, especially for the elderly and the sick. The days, months and years go by too quickly, without us realizing it. This feeling is proof that our mind has lost the original balance of when we were young. Indeed, if we remember, time had much more value when we were young and we could managed to do a lot more in that time.

The rapid recovery of that wonderful feeling of a time of which we are exclusive owners, of a time that passes, but slowly and in a productive manner (**recovering also intelligence**), is the peculiarity of fasting without water and with natural food. You can avoid drinking, but I succeeded only for four days. And it was a very tough. Ohsawa wrote that a man could live without water for ten whole days! Me no! I had to try it because, after many days of fasting with water, I still had diarrhoea. Fasting four days without drinking, I managed to stop a diarrhoea that was unstoppable by any other means. On the fourth day, I looked at my wall clock and saw the second hand go by terribly slowly!

Time, when fasting without water, stops, no longer passes, we become the present and everything we do is full of meaning. My mind was clearer than ever and incredibly, in just four days, I had recovered the physical energy that even after three years of intense sport I could not have achieved (I know what I am talking about because I have done a lot of sport). Be careful though: fasting without water gets tougher as the time goes on. On the fourth day, your heart races like a Ferrari, even if you are in bed. I do not know if everyone is up to this challenge! However, fasting without water raises our immune defences to a maximum, in just four days. Very important at the end of fasting is not to lose your head. Avoid too much fruit, which quenches your thirst even more than water. It is better to extend the obtained benefits a little more by making an effort to drink only a little water for at least one more day.

After the third day of fasting, with water, I began to vomit several times a day, for six days. I expelled terrible substances of a dark colour I think, but I could not get the desired healing results, despite going at it for nine days in a row. However, fasting with water, considering its cleansing action, especially for the stomach, was an excellent preparation for fasting without water.

My Story in a Nutshell: Medical Scams

At age five, I got sick of very strong allergies and allergic rhinitis. I sneezed all the time and went through ten handkerchiefs a day with my nose often stuffy nose and inflamed. At eight years old, I was already taking eight antihistamine tablets a day, and for this reason I was constantly very drowsy. Can you imagine how it feels to be a child and drowsy all the time, especially when you need to study? Do you know how it feels to suffer a constantly blocked, runny and inflamed nose, even at night, for months on end?

At the age of sixteen, I weighed 63kg (at 1.73 metres tall) and I was in good shape, despite the occasional allergy and asthma. Then, one day, I happened to read about an American diet, one used by astronauts, a diet with a system of points, and I fantasized about getting into better shape than I was.

I thus began to eliminate cereals, which according to the diet were fattening, and devoted myself to eating only meat and carrots. In a month I lost two to three kilograms, but suddenly began to feel bad. Indeed, I had developed a strong colitis. It served no purpose to start eating pasta again, the colitis had settled in with strong spasms and a lot of mucus with troublesome stools.

The gastroenterologist I turned to, instead of asking me what had happened and what I had been eating, subjected me to my first painful colonoscopy (at eighteen years old), which **of**

course did not turn up anything unusual. The prescribed cure was lactic cultures and intestinal motility depressants.

These medicines worsen my state even more and, due to the intestinal motility drugs, I began to lie down on my bed exhausted in the afternoon, with 120 heartbeats per minute. And the lactic enzymes did not change anything. Naturally, I went back again and again to the same doctor, who eventually refused to see me. But we had for the appointments handsomely, I had undertaken that awful medical exam and I had taken the prescribed medicines. How was it possible that nothing had changed, that I was still suffering despite it all? Was he not a doctor that specialist? How was it possible that I was still unwell?

Of course, after some years of continuously feeling bad, my father looked for another doctor and found an eminent gastroenterologist in Bologna. To cut a long story short, even this eminent doctor prescribed me lactic enzymes, but of another kind, and other motility depressants. But once again the drugs produced no improvement, I continued to suffer and to bombard the doctor with phone calls so that shortly after, like the previous one, he dumped me too, and despite the significant amount of money my father had handed over for that twenty-minute appointment. I was obviously outraged. How was it possible to pay all that money and not obtain even the slightest result? At the time, I did not know doctors well enough and I learnt only over time. But I was thinking that if an engineer builds a house that then collapses, he goes to jail. So how was it possible that these doctors had cheated me but could not be sent to jail? Doctors treat people, but how many people actually heal with their medicine?

Colonoscopy is only a test, it doesn't cure anyone or anything.

The patient has to take a laxative the day before, in the evening, to completely empty the intestine. Under these conditions, the following morning, the patient undergoes the examination, which consists in inserting a flexible tube into the intestine, up from the bottom for about 2-3 metres. On the tip of the tube is a tiny video camera, with which the doctor observes and photographs the intestinal walls. On the tip there is also a gripper, to do a biopsy, which means that **the gastroenterologist uses the gripper to rip off pieces from the intestinal mucous membrane**. These will then be examined in a lab to determine if there are any tumours or anything else harmful present.

The presence of tumours or diverticulitis are much rarer in the young, to my knowledge, than colitis. So, given the ease with which gastroenterologists induce patients to undergo this painful and traumatizing examination, I would like to know, over a thousand tests, how many are positive for tumours or diverticulitis.

In these cases, physicians argue that there is the subsequent need for surgical removal (they really claim this, see chapter on 'Important News').

The three colonoscopies that doctors convinced me to undergo, despite being strongly opposed, did not lead to any useful result whatsoever. Indeed, there was no sign either of diverticulitis or tumours, and the medical analysis returned "nervous nonspecific colitis", which meant practically that I had suffered for absolutely nothing and had no help in finding a cure. I wonder, how much is a doctor's fee (paid for by the state) to perform a colonoscopy?

Towards twenty-four years old, to my severe colitis was added a trivial urethritis, which, however, was not as trivial as all that. Despite the urethral swabs, the hospital laboratory indicating staphylococcus, the antibiogram indicating which antibiotics were effective and which were not, the antibiotics I took did not cure me. The expert medical dialectic (doctors are very good at charming people with words) justified the failure of the antibiotic therapy with the term "antibiotic resistant", but this does not justify the facts.

I went on with these tremendous antibiotic treatments for more than eight months, without the slightest improvement. In the end, I decided to keep the infection as it was and swallow any more antibiotics, but I necessarily had to start thinking about how else I was going to get better, because the pain was unbearable. I had also hassled my general practitioner, but I began to realize that going to a doctor was just a waste of time and that medicines do not cure anything. How many people in the world are in these conditions is a mystery to me, because I really cannot conceive how many people are genuinely cured by going to the doctor, and I do not understand how primary care physicians and specialists alike still enjoy so much respect. The fact is that there is a strong demand on the internet for information on how to recover from various diseases. I realized this by observing the number of visits to the small website that I had set up, http://guariremangiando.it, through reports that Google Analytics supplied me with. Unfortunately, only recently I closed down the site. Perhaps many people don't know where to turn, having wandered away unsatisfied from their duty-doctor. I believe so, evidence being my forty-five years of experience with doctors and medicines vainly hoping to find something that is a bit more than an expensive and often harmful temporary remedy.

But today, after the many twists and turns with doctors, after years of fruitless searching for cures for one or another reason, I have arrived at a certain shore. Having tried everything, from herbal medicine to homeopathy, yoga, quack healers, priests and blessings, various hygienist therapies, raw food diets and fasting, today I have some certainty, which has also become a source of happiness, because I have discovered the power of nutrition not only as a real cure for diseases of the intestine, but as a treatment for the entire body, including teeth and sight. Indeed, nutrition is not a medicine, which makes claims on targeting a single disorder. No, nutrition does a lot more, it involves the whole body and totally transform the life of a person.

Nutrition is also a real cure for infections and I think it is fundamental for curing any disease, precisely because it involves the whole body. We are sick of too much (unnatural) food!

Stop suffering without medicines, in just a few days

In 2001 or so, I returned from a trip abroad where I contracted a double infection, of the intestine (I had something like white thread-like grains of rice in my faeces) and the urethra. Years before I had been able to put a stop to urethritis through the right diet, but I was still not an expert at the time and I had lost my way a little. Now, I was forced into semi-fasting, because the two infections this time were truly terrible. I began to eat very little and only boiled spinach and a little pasta. Why? Simply because I still had in mind Ohsawa's book "The Macrobiotic Diet" and, convinced that only eating rice would not be good for me, I chose pasta and added spinach because Ohsawa throughout his book said that life is made up of at least two elements. So if he said to eat only rice, then one other element had to be missing!

I chose spinach and not rice but pasta, which I perceived as much more suitable and curative. **In addition, with a dual infection in progress, I immediately realized that any other food I ate, though little, would make the pain unbearable!** Just spinach and a little pasta allowed me to hold on without seeking out a doctor! I had bean-like foreign material in my stool and white pus dripped from my penis, all day and night! Forgive me for the details but it is better to know than be ignorant of the facts! The whole thing lasted more than a month. In anguish I returned to Italy, very thin, and almost immediately I went to a natural health centre near Venice, which gave no results. But remembering that long before I almost completely stopped the urethritis in its tracks, I thought about that diet and I began to eat just pasta and spinach, a little something sweet for breakfast and almost nothing else. In less than ten days I was completely cured!

I could only eat spinach and pasta, without feeling too much pain, four or five forks of spinach and four or five forks of pasta, as if the food was like a medicine to be taken in small doses, as if in this way it would only nourish my body and not the sickness, with the food not having time to get to the sickness due to it being metabolized and absorbed by the body before. And so the sickness began to die, so to speak, of hunger. I was suffering a lot and so I held in there as much as I could in eating little. Then, suddenly, one day, I was rewarded for my efforts. My sight (at the time I had to wear glasses) began to get clearer and clearer and, to my delight, I realized that the diet was working and it was also curing my myopia! I went on as long as I could eating just a little spinach and pasta and I finally managed to get the better of the two infections of the intestine and the urethra. The pain of the double infection ceased as if by magic and I recovered several grades of sight, from 4 to 9 in the right eye, despite being perpetually short-sighted since childhood. I had cured myself, alone, by eating, with no medicine and no doctor.

Since then, I have had no more asthma, allergies, otitis or herpes. Two weeks ago my partner had a bit of herpes, but I kissed her the same and did not contract herpes again.

The satisfaction was immense and I talked it over with my parents. There was still one problem, the colitis, which was difficult to eradicate, because at the time I did not have the knowledge that I developed in the following years. I began to eat poorly again, and did not eat meat or fish but ate a lot of rice, cheese and vegetables. And I appealed to a doctor (a public specialist) once again for mood disorders. I was given a drug, Z*******a, and in no time at all my colitis had become a terrible diarrhoea with different alternating phases that arrived at as many as fifteen discharges per day (for years). I will not speak of the other side effects from which I was greatly damaged or of the other drugs and medical specialists, a real torture lasting thirteen years, because it is too hard for me to tell it all, but know that this particular drug has undergone a class-action in the United States, where thousands of people have been compensated, while in Italy the drug is still prescribed as if safe. My life was devastated, I could hardly leave the house, it was unthinkable. That drug and the others made me go crazy and I went through some terrible years. Eventually, I managed to sort myself out by changing my diet with a huge effort and countless attempts. To-day, and only fairly recently, I have finally discovered the power of fish, cabbage, wheat pasta, buckwheat, aubergine, potatoes and just a little spinach. These are the fundamental foods for healing! I have discovered that there are foods that really can cure, but I have also learned to be cautious. When you feel good, your diet must be often varied. We have to vary foods almost every day, because many diseases settle into the body in long periods of poor diet. When a disease settles in, only eating a lit-tle and only two or three elements can change the situation. This has been my experience, better than any medicine, kinder than any doctor, my personal experience, the ability to cope with the problems of life by my strength alone and then the great satisfaction of telling others. This knowledge is what I try am trying to convey to all. I really hope that there are others that can quickly draw the fantastic benefits that I have from the right dietary efforts. I have gained an awareness and now I have a mission to accomplish: to ferry as many people as possible to the other side of the river.

For natural medicine, whose founders were Lezaeta and Ohsawa, all diseases have a single source: the intestines, the stomach and what we put into it. I totally agree. We do not need dairy products for essential calcium. This is given to us by fish, which is fundamental as a food. Also, dairy products and eggs are bacteriologically packed with microbial life. Cooked vegeta-bles, cereals and fruits have virtually zero. I should point out here, though, that I do not believe in vegetarianism. Animal products do have qualities, but fish above all. In the presence of an infection avoid all dairy products, eggs, bananas, too much meat and especially too much cereal, lots of vegetables and too much food in general.

Dairy products benefit nerves and skin. But if your children are restless, agitated, if they have problems at school, the cause lies in too much meat and too many dairy products. Too much milk for breakfast, yoghurt, ice-cream and cheese. It is too much for their bodies and probably they do not eat enough cooked vegetables!

For natural medicine there are not different types of colitis, only varying degrees of severity (e.g. ulcerative colitis is a colitis, but only more severe than other forms). Just as there are not hundreds of different diseases, but only diseases of one organ rather than another (Yin or Yang diseases). In most diseases the real cause is food and therefore it is only food that can heal. My story is the self-evident demonstration. That is why what can cure teeth can cure even bones, because bones and teeth are both made of the same stuff. But what cures bones and teeth also helps other organs and thus cures various diseases, which often occur simultaneously in a sick body. Once foods that your body does not tolerate well have been identified, it is easy to switch to other foods, but knowledge requires practice and observation of your body. Learning to observe is critical for healing.

In addition to limiting the quantity that you eat, you need to know that you must eat only one vegetable and one animal protein in each single meal.

When you go to the doctor and ask for a cure for herpes, the doctor prescribes a cream, that twenty years ago cost 24,000 Lira (about 15 Euros today) for just three grams! And this cream had absolutely no effect. And today?

When you go to a specialist gastroenterologist, you pay a minimum of 150 Euros, for a twenty-minute visit. For colitis they prescribe drugs such as lactic enzymes and intestinal motility depressants. But who, I ask, has ever obtained anything positive from these drugs?

When you go to a specialist in allergies, after the various allergen sensitivity tests, the prescribe antihistamines, whose effect lasts a few hours, maybe more, but then the allergy comes back and you have to pop another pill. The same applies for asthma. Then, most antihistamines cause severe drowsiness. How many of you are happy with this?

When you go to the dentist for an abscess, the dentist may prescribe antibiotics before treating the tooth. How many days or weeks you have been forced to follow antibiotic treatment? And when you went back to the dentist did the tooth still hurt? After how many days did the pain go away? In the case of periodontal disease or periodontitis, what medications ever cured you completely? Or is it progressive, unstoppable?

Has a the pain of tooth decay ever just gone away without the dentist? It has happened to me, just by eliminating dairy products and meat from my diet and replacing them with fish, cabbage, aubergine and bread or pasta.

Have you ever solved the problem of bleeding gums or sensitive teeth with mouthwash alone?

Have you really ever had gastritis that was cured with medication? How long have you had to take antibiotics and anti-inflammatory drugs to cure cystitis?

For an ear infection how much have you paid a specialist? How long did it take for you to get over it with the prescribed antibiotic treatment?

Have those with diabetes ever been able to lower their blood sugar with medication alone?
Has your doctor ever prescribed antibiotics or other drugs, or tests without any warning of the pain involved, all resulting in a worsening of your condition, without any possibility of complaint or compensation?

Due to several psychiatric drugs, I had the following dental problems: tooth decay, periodontal disease (and yellowed teeth due to antibiotic treatments), neuralgia, abscesses, bleeding gums for years, moving teeth, decalcified teeth and teeth sensitive to cold, water and touch! But I saved my teeth with my diet!

Herpes.
I believe herpes to be caused by peanuts (and too many sausages). When you puncture a herpetic bubble with a pointed instrument liquid comes out. With some cotton wool, dab a bit of alcohol on three or four times a day for three or four days, avoiding the above mentioned foods and meat leads to an easy recovery.

Observations on antibiotics:
the mechanism of the cleansing diet and the importance of hunger

What are the logical and scientific proofs that antibiotics specifically attack pathogenic bacteria in the sick body? There aren't any! How can it be shown that a poison (the antibiotic) inside our body attacks bacteria? How can it be proved? It is absolutely impossible. Indeed, if anything, it has been shown that the sick who take antibiotics feel worse. The human body reacts immediately to any attack, any poisoning or intoxication, first of all trying with all its strength to neutralize the attack of those harmful substances. But in so doing it gets tired and weak! What is a bacterial load anyway? It is a group of bacteria that comes from nothing else but food! The bacteria and their mucous come from dairy products, first of all, in the stomach and intestines and, then, circulating throughout the entire body, with ability to settle in and damage any organ or tissue, including even bones and teeth. Staphylococcus come from dairy products! Phlegm, mucous and pus come from dairy products! But dairy products can also act as incubators for millions of other different types of bacteria! How do bacteria become pathogenic? By heat and when the body is weak with an almost occult indigestion, when the body is unable to expel through faeces the excess of foods in the gut. There is too much, the body fails to contain it all and it begins to migrate from the gut, multiplying because the body cannot control its growth. It invades the rest of the body, damaging the other organs. The attack on peripheral organs, in my opinion, is linked to the nervous system, which is fed primarily by cereals. Too much cereal can aggravate an infection or toothache. To pour bleach into a bag of rotting waste might do something to kill bacteria, but the human body is not a sack of garbage, it is alive. To say that a poison can decrease the bacterial load, which is nothing but FOOD decomposing inside the body, most likely caused by bad digestion, is nonsense and a lie! If it is food, logic says it must be re-eaten by part of the body (no longer through the mouth), must be metabolized and the rest must leave the body as faeces. Therefore hunger (and a natural detoxifying diet) helps the body to cleanse itself of the food residues. Fatigue is a sign that the immune system is less active, at its weakest! The weak, the powerless, the weary and the stressed are more susceptible to disease! And they are never truly hungry, they only indulge mental desires.

If you are under antibiotic treatment can you spend time in the sun? The answer is NO! Why? Because antibiotics weaken the immune system and increase sensitivity so that even the normally beneficial sun's rays can become harmful! The sick do not need to become weaker but rather stronger, more resistant! More awake and smarter! Happier! Not constantly a wreck! Nature heals us by making us stronger, not weaker, by curing acute symptoms, not giving us others, by increasing well-being, not sickness, by returning energy to us and not by taking it away.

Antibiotics are not cures! Antibiotics, like psychiatric drugs, like other poisons liberally distributed by drug peddlers, harm you and do not cure a damn thing!

The first assumption of Science is that it must respect and respond to, before anything else, logic! If something is not logical, then it is not science because there is no proof! And there is the DECEPTION! If a drug weakens me (though I am not up to date on what exists on the market today, such as the sulphonamides and antibiotics I took since I was a child, even for a banal flu), then it is not medicine but poison.

If a food or a drug is a toxin, we cannot simultaneously consider it a cure, it is one or the other! Science does not admit ambiguity, this is a cardinal principle, fundamental. Food, though, can be harmful at a certain time, and then, once cured, it can become neutral. But this is not true for drugs, which are not foods, they harm you and take away energy. If other sicknesses occur, we must be immediately be alarmed and avoid taking the drugs. Moreover, why extract from food its active ingredients to create a drug? If they are already present in the right dose and form as intended by our Creator! Just for profit it seems. Why not analyze the real healing ability of that food on the human body, perhaps in combination with other foods? Extracting ingredients from food is a fruitless activity, there is nothing really to sell and nothing to gain! From the point of view of natural medicine, as I understand it (in which five or six foods are all we need to cure ourselves), identifying thousands of different diseases is misleading and leads only to nonsense and false ideologies that bring confusion, uncertainty and fear. And it is not true that stress and anxieties make us sick (with colitis, gastritis, mental illness, etc.). A healthy man does not get sick for stress, fear or anxiety. The healthy body is strong, durable and naturally has a healthy mind. An intoxicated and weak body is what results in a weak mind, fear and anxiety.

You cannot convince the body with words, you cannot cure the mind with words!

But the mind and body respond like clockwork to a vegetarian bipolar diet or a natural diet (with fish, cereals and little else), resulting in happy and intelligent people!

In January 2014, I was still suffering from diarrhoea! I had been suffering from it for years. In August or September 2013, I went to live in a new home. My partner, Katya, took me every week to a Ukrainian 'mix-market' to buy sauerkraut, which she then cooked with meat. I slowly began to feel some improvement in my hitherto uncontrollable diarrhoea. It was November, and after about a month of eating sauerkraut frequently, one day I had the idea of replacing it with its fresh component cabbage. So I began to cook the cabbage alone, with just a little oil, a brief browning over a low heat for ten to fifteen minutes, with a little water and salt. And it worked. In about twenty days, despite still smoking ten cigarettes a day and drinking coffee, known to aggravate diarrhoea, I went from fifteen discharges to three or four. The improvement was evident! A cure for disease through food and without medicine! My dream, from 1998, of healing through select foods was coming true. In February, I began to speak fluently again and partially stopped violently grinding my teeth. This effect had been caused by the psychiatric drugs that I had been obliged to take since 2006 and which devastated my health. But as the diarrhoea stopped, over about a month, I began to get swollen legs and ankles. Initially, I did not make anything of it, but gradually I got to the point of not being able to walk, except for short stretches. My skin became very white and sensitive to the sun, loose and baggy over my muscles, which had almost shrunk away. One fine day, on 5th March 2014, in a programme called "Le Iene" on the television channel Italia 1, they broadcast the story of a man who could no longer stand chemotherapy and cured himself of a brain cancer in metastases by only drinking blended vegetable juice. I immediately jumped up from my seat! I knew a lot more about it than a mere blend of bitter green leaves, and I had tried it all out already, if without an adequate complementary diet. For years and years now I had been curing many ills simply by avoiding certain foods and favouring others. And in the past I had tried blended juices, even if briefly. With the knowledge that I had acquired over the years, from macrobiotics to naturism, it made me realise that now was the time to write, now was the big moment I had dreamed so much of. On 10th March, I began to put all I could think of that had been effective directly onto the internet. With my cabbage cure, I had more energy and I began to wake up during the night and from one to four a.m., inspired, I wrote. Today is 19th August (though the correction of this book I am doing over January 2015, I am leaving in these earlier dates because they are a good reference). It took a little over four months to finally feel better and today I am happy. The healing of my body gave way, at the beginning of March, to a significant healing of my mind and memory and the rewards are still coming daily. Unlike fasting, which is great, especially if you do it almost spontaneously like children, curing yourself with the right diet does not necessarily produce immediately extraordinary results, but will cure you if you find the right combination.

An Anecdote

Around the year 1984, I heard on the radio (while working in the photography shop of my mother) a transmission on Radio MM which talked of colitis. A new cure was being publicized by the radio speaker and owner of the radio station, who was a psychiatrist named E*******i, very famous in the city. He was proposing new pills, coming, I believe, from England, to permanently cure colitis! Some days later, I turned up in this famous city clinic, where the man had his studio. In two minutes flat, not a second more, he gave me the name of this miracle drug and presented me with the price tag: 150,000 Lira! In 1984! That is equivalent to 80 Euros today!
I paid up, but he gave me no receipt. Just as I was leaving, however, a poor boy of no more than twenty years old saved my life. He was waiting to get into the studio right after me and I saw him amble forward in a state of fear, swaying visibly, out of his wits, evidently under the spell of these harmful pharmaceutical drugs! So, I ended up not taking that medicine, I persevered with my colitis and silently thanked God for putting that poor boy across my way.

As recounted above, once I had stopped having diarrhoea my ankles became swollen and this I put down to the fact that I was no longer discharging all the accumulated toxins, almost certainly of the many psychiatric drugs that I had been obliged to take. To reduce the swelling in my ankles and legs, I reduced my intake of vegetables, both raw and cooked. But I continued to eat a lot of meat and cabbage. I still had not the clear vision that I have now. I had to remind myself of when I had urethritis and ate mainly fish with little else, suddenly feeling better. However, this time it was not enough. I began to read and reread Ohsawa's book "The Macrobiotic Diet" and finally one day I began to understand what was hidden between the lines. Everything began to come together in my mind. It all began from the fact that fruit had temporarily cured my colitis (perhaps in 1998, I went to a hygienist centre in Treviso, where I ate only fruit for six days). But this was a very difficult cure and brought with it extremely undesirable mental side effects (I developed a harmfully absurd and irrepressible energy). If fruit was a starting point, then it was certainly wrong to think that cereals alone were the solution (fruit and cereals are opposites on the acid-base scale). There had to be a middle way. I understood only after many attempts and still months of severe stomach-aches, in short, because my memories had steamed up, but then I remembered fish and my grandfather, our conversations, my first fasting at his house, my first healing. Of course, then it was the fasting that cured me, but it was reinforced immediately after by eating fish.

For me, healing passes through at least three phases: emptying of the rectum, maintenance of the empty rectum and finally reduction in the inflammation of the rectum and colon just above. The diffusion of these effects to the other organs of the body finally allows them to offload their bacterial content, which before constituted disease manifested in a plurality of symptoms from the most varied names. If the sick person, immediately after his rectum has emptied, starts to eat the same foods that have sustained until now his illness, he will lose any benefit of the food and will instantly return to suffering. The more ancient the ill, the most polluted is our bodily landscape, and the longer it takes the sick person to heal. But do not despair, because the body is not a mathematician.
In my experience infections, allergies, asthma and gastritis were cured after days of dietary constancy with the appropriate food. And the cure came without warning, suddenly I was healed. In the case of my colitis it was different because colitis is really difficult to heal, at least for me it was so. Changing the intestinal flora of bacteria and microorganisms requires healthy food and reduced quantities.

That is the reason for these combinations:
Fish and pasta
Cabbage with pasta and fruit
Cabbage with pasta
Fish with fruit, why not?
Spinach with pasta
Aubergine with fish and/or pasta

Eating nothing else in the same meal and maintain the same dietary combination for several days really helps, in my humble opinion, with many difficult diseases, from colitis to toothache! You cannot beat or destroy bacteria! If they are in your stomach, causing gastritis, you just need a little fish to change the pH to neutral! But if they are deeply entrenched in the intestines and organs, the only thing you can do is calm them down, removing their nourishment, which makes them aggressive and fearsome, and accompany them safely out of the body! When even little food becomes too much, then it is a sign that you should fast, because sometimes even good food is too much, **for example, when you have a high temperature**. Bacteria are stronger and more resistant when they feed on natural sugars, which can also come from cooked vegetables and fruit.

I noticed while eating certain cooked vegetables, aubergine, cooked cabbage and buckwheat that **the tartar on my teeth reduced visibly in just a few days and with a pair of scissors I was able to remove it easily from my teeth**. However, I also noted that cooked vegetables, buckwheat and potatoes soon make you put on weight if you eat them too frequently and without fruit or fish. I was very bloated, especially at my belly and ankles, but I had not been eating fish! When I decided to leave aside the cooked vegetables and dedicate my diet to fish, finally the swelling went down in my legs.

Reflecting on the food habits of people who live in hot climates, where there is no sea or farming, I remembered that their main nourishment is based on cereals, fruit and sour curdled milk, i.e. ricotta or cottage cheese! Under the scorching sun, at 40-50 degrees, they eat at night only (and this could be a problem that leads to disease, above all mental, sleeping with a full stomach!) and almost exclusively cereals, fruit, ricotta and fresh cheese! But they rarely eat cooked vegetables because they increase the feeling of warmth! And the peoples of the South, though mostly lean and agile, have many dental and mental health problems (as all those who eat dairy products inappropriately). That is the downside of dairy products. Mozzarella cheese, for example, refreshes the body from the heat and protects skin from the sun. But too many fresh dairy products, being in time harmful for the mind and the teeth above all, should always be alternated with fish, which leads to neutrality in the body.

Chemicals are used more and more in agriculture and the food industry. In advertisements they promise that certain lactic bacteria are good for colitis and diarrhoea when actually they cause them. They promise miracle cures for gastritis. They promise mouthwashes that cure the bleeding of gums. They promise definitive cures for headaches, diarrhoea and rhinitis. But these conditions derive from the preservatives in sausages, bakery products and confectionery, in sterilized milk and dairy products. From hormones and antibiotics in the meat of animals from when they were still alive. From pesticides used in agriculture. From hens that produce *chemical* eggs. Did you know that in Italy there are almost no more bees left? Did you know that in the sunflower fields of Italy there no more sparrows, while in poorer Eastern Europe they still have to use scarecrows?

I had several moments of healing from eating only fruit for six days. It was always a very strong experience and difficult to achieve. It takes a very determined mind to eat just one or two fruits twice a day and nothing else! With a balanced diet it is easier, but takes longer and you have to choose the most appropriate food day by day. However, **with the dietary method you have to prepare with your evening meal your healing for the next morning. Indeed, I believe that it is very effective to skip dinner altogether.** Or rather, if you eat sensibly at dinner, you have less air at night and you begin to reduce discharges in the morning. This is the first important sign that makes it clear you are on the right track. Everything should be repeated, keeping in mind that healing does not happen just with an expulsion from the intestine.

Constipation is, however, a sign of healing. The colon begins to reduce its inflammation from the rectum, which is the lowest point, and slowly the healing proceeds upwards. To understand this alone all you have to do is observe your body daily during your controlled diet, or fasting or semi-fasting. And with a reduction in inflammation, you will get simultaneous relief for your head, including your teeth!

With a natural and bipolar diet, without medication, I cured myself of all of the following:

Allergies and asthma, lasting 34 and 36 years respectively.

A initially constipated severe nonspecific colitis, lasting 22 years (and chronic diarrhoea 12 years).

An otitis and recurrent parotitis lasting for many years.

Painful and movable teeth (which were strengthened with the cure and I no longer go to the dentist), periodontal disease, bleeding gums, tartar (I only had to observe my teeth in the mirror every day to see the improvement, the tartar coming off with the slight pressure of tweezers and the nicotine stains disappearing gradually) and yellow teeth (that became white again).

Chronic urethritis from antibiotic-resistant staphylococcus (lasting 8 years, despite antibiotic and anti-inflammatory treatment).

Myopia (I had 4/10 in my right eye and an obligation to wear glasses for driving, now no longer an obligation).

Severe gastritis (cured by eating mostly boiled fish and cooked vegetables).

Schizophrenia (my diagnosis was changed to 'schizoaffective disorder', of which nothing remains and I no longer take any psycho-active drugs).

Herpes of the lips and nose, which lasted a year and was drug-resistant.

Warts on the hands, arthritis of the wrists and neck and back pain due to herniated discs.

Terrible swelling in the ankles.

Whatever disease you have, change your diet by eliminating first of all sausages and all dairy products. Eliminate foods that are harmful for you (harmful for you even if you haven't yet noticed). Or if you do not improve just with these changes in your diet, then follow my instructions for semi-fasting, which is the only easy, sustainable, real and effective therapy.

Eat little, only two or three select foods for seven to ten days!

For natural medicine, which is the only true medicine, the name of the disease is of no importance, only the organ in question. Thus generic colitis, Crohn's disease and any type of colitis, including rectal ulcerative, collagenous, viral, spastic, anxious, ischemic, lymphocytic, micro-erosive, traveller and so on can all be cured in the same way. The same goes for gastritis, proctitis, etc. And for hay-fever, pollen allergy and contact allergies. And for cystitis, urethritis, prostatitis, asthma, asthmatic bronchitis, flu, pneumonia, etc. And, naturally, the cure is different if you are constipated or have diarrhoea, so choose the foods and cooking method that work for you.

Cabbage cooked (for 10 to 15 minutes) with a little water and a little olive oil is the king of natural medicines (and works great for chronic fatigue). However, it is not true that all vegetables have the same healing effect on the body and mind. In my experience (and according to the famous French herbalist Jean Valnet), cabbage is the most important natural medicine that nature provides us with. To verify this personally you need only adopt it, for at least for two weeks, in a very simple bipolar diet that consists of eating only two foods in each single meal, for example, cooked vegetables (of which cabbage is the most curative) with a choice of cereal. **Buckwheat is very curative for the pancreas because it lowers blood sugar**, but not so good together with cabbage because it brings on swelling. Or you can try a cooked vegetable with boiled fish instead of cereal. For example, pasta and cooked cabbage is a great combination for many health problems. And you can alternate cabbage with spinach, aubergine or some other vegetable. You could also try to see the effects of simply introducing cabbage into your normal diet two or three times a week, without making any other changes. Those who suffer from teeth problems (caries, pain, tartar, bleeding gums, periodontal disease) or diarrhoea will soon realize its effect, especially if they eat it at dinner. In very painful and acute inflammatory diseases such as infections, diarrhoea, colitis, cystitis, urethritis and other diseases, the quantities are very important. You must eat just a little cabbage and cereals (fish is useful especially for infections) with the aim to develop over a few days a slight feeling of hunger, which needs to be maintained for the whole two weeks of this diet (which can be extended if you want without issue).

Only two weeks is what it takes and then you can vary your diet by replacing, for example, cabbage with fruit or other cooked or raw vegetables such as spinach, grilled aubergine, salad or chicory. Or even during the first two weeks, of course, you can replace the cabbage with some grilled aubergine or other boiled vegetable.

Eating only two or three foods per meal, the sick person patient can learn which foods are good for him and which are not. Just remember what you ate the day before to understand if that food made you better or worse and act accordingly by keeping it in or eliminating it from your diet. When you are healthy you can eat anything, but when you are sick, in order to heal, you need to limit yourself to food that is as natural as possible, including meat and fish, which are natural foods with specific actions!

Meat can help the heart, but it can stimulate sexual activity excessively. Fish is vital to regulate stomach acid for those who have gastritis, infections and most likely many other ills. Naturally, meat should only be used for short periods of time and in small quantities. Because vegetarians are happier and smarter!

In the South of the world people eat lots of fruit because it is refreshing. In the North people eat more cooked vegetables, which are warming but make you put on weight. In the North people eat more meat, in the South more fish. It is very important for the sick to avoid eating only pasta or rice for weeks. It is better to alternate them often.

For two weeks, if you really wish to improve your condition, you need to avoid most of all meat, all dairy products, milk, yoghurt, ice-cream, kefir, butter, cream, eggs, yeast, all leavened foods such as bread, cakes and pizza, especially if you have allergy problems or asthma, snacks (though chocolate for me is allowed), beer and mushrooms (yeast is also a fungus and the beer is produced with yeast), which are harmful for asthmatics, honey, canned foods, frozen vegetables, cold meats and sausages, puffed rice, whole grains, too much food at breakfast, too much meat, too much food in general, two different cereals in the same meal and too much coffee (coffee can harm the heart - try giving it up for three days and you will notice the difference!).
Honey in tea easily provokes gastritis. Chilli with cereals also.

Raw vegetables especially, but also cooked, should never be eaten in the morning, before 11.30 am. In the morning, it is okay to have a little coffee with a piece of cake. Raw vegetables (e.g. onions), in my experience, eaten in the morning can provoke **sudden neuralgia!**
Anyhow, raw vegetables can also be very beneficial (even though personally I have not used them to cure myself). But those who have intestinal problems and are overweight must be careful, and should avoid too much meat, substituting it with fish. Bulgur wheat, what Moldovans call Arnautka, is similar to couscous, but I believe is better and tastes great. As I recall, many years ago I read that it has a slight antibiotic effect, especially in the case of cystitis and disease of the lungs and bronchi, or airways. You can try it as a first course. Be careful, however, if you have colitis, swelling or toothache, for which I do not recommend it at all! As I would not recommend whole-grain cereals either.

We can let ourselves be guided by instinct, but always remember that **the instinct of the sick is fallacious**. This is because it leads to those foods that are bad for us, at least until we have some experience with natural dieting, which means, I repeat, eliminating all that has been transformed by man, all dairy products (in nature, no animal whatsoever returns to mother milk after weaning) and all craft and industrial food.

If, during your dietary changes or semi-fasting, you become constipated, you should definitely not worry, because constipation is part of the healing process, which takes several days. The rectum becomes clean, acute pain will cease and slowly the healing process will start from the lowest point of your body and move upwards. So if you cannot defecate, you absolutely must not be alarmed.

If you have allergies, you have probably done tests to determine what you are allergic to, but the tests cannot always identify the exact cause of your allergy. For example, many years ago I did the lactose-lactulose test, which, for me, did not indicate any specific allergies to dairy products. **However, after each subsequent asthmatic crisis, I began to pay attention to what I had eaten the day before and I was able to understand which foods triggered the asthma: above all dairy products, beer and some sausages. Eliminating these foods for a long time, I eliminated permanently from my life my asthma and allergies, and today I can once again eat those foods, but without any crisis.**

In particular, for allergies and asthma (and bronchopulmonary infections) especially avoid all dairy products, ice-cream, cheese, yoghurt, etc., which are the primary cause of allergies, asthma, bronchial pulmonary infections and many other diseases, and cured meats, **sausages**, beer, mushrooms, canned foods, **too much meat**, **bread**, yeast and leavened products. The time required to see the first results depends on how you follow these guidelines. It could be a month, maybe sooner, then the asthma and allergy will disappear.

Use my method: if today you had an asthma attack or an allergic reaction, try to remember what you ate yesterday and avoid it, until you are cured!

In general, when you are in a lot of pain:
Eat little at breakfast and skip your evening meal.

For gastritis, eat boiled fish for several days. Eat only boiled fish and cooked cabbage for various meals. Even frozen fish is okay. And as well as cooked cabbage, you can use aubergine, etc.

Avoid all dairy products, bread, cakes, unhealthy lard, fried lard, mushrooms, gravies, not fresh tomato sauces, wine, preserved foods, frozen vegetables, wholegrain cereals at breakfast, puffed rice, two cereals at the same meal, snacks, panettone, pandoro, chocolate, non-genuine sausages and spicy foods. **Tea with honey, drank frequently over a long period will cause gastritis, as well as the chilli with cereals (rice or pasta).**
Let us talk a little about the quality of food we eat in Italy. Some time ago I happened to put some pork fat on the stove to make it brown and crispy in order to add some flavour to a plate of pasta. After a while, the smoke rising from the pan was smelly and black. And I didn't fancy eating it anymore. Instead, another day, after putting into the same pan some pork fat from another foreign country, I observed that there was no smell or black smoke and we ate our great tasting pasta in fine company.

Colitis can be constipated or diarrheal with, depending on the severity, the presence of air, mucous, blood and strong spasms. In my opinion drugs are ineffective.
Changing some foods in your diet is the most effective, but it certainly can take some time to manifest its power. However, do not despair and only eat pasta with cooked vegetables. Fish can also help. Avoid most meat, all dairy products and too much food. The more strict you are with your diet, the faster you will see the benefits. Eat little fruit.

Semi-fasting with fruit (my 6 days are a credible figure for many illnesses) can give excellent results for many different illnesses including colitis, cystitis, otitis, parotitis, proctitis, arthritis, toothache, urethritis, asthma, skin diseases, gastritis, etc. It is only a few days, compared to years or a lifetime of suffering. I know that it is extremely difficult, but I advise you to try it out (even if just for a few days). It takes a bit of determination and courage, but you will see that nothing bad will happen. For sure, though, the bipolar diet is a lot easier!
Fruit is not a daily medicine, in the sense that it is no use to eat fruit at the end of a normal meal. Fruit has an incredible power, but only if eaten as the only food for several days. It practically allows the body to eliminate years of toxic residues left inside you, which are the cause of a plurality of acute symptoms associated with the names of the most various diseases. No drug can do this, but semi-fasting with fruit or with vegetables and cereals can. Years ago I beat colitis (do you know anyone that beat colitis?) in this way: I ate only fruit for six days in a hygienist therapy centre and managed to normalize colitis.

For diarrhoea it is absolutely necessary to semi-fast with fruit, or cooked cabbage, fish, pasta or buckwheat.

For cystitis and urethritis, it is the same diet as for colitis.
Cystitis is a painful condition. It burns painfully when you urinate and you may have to urinate many times a day. I don't quite recall exactly which vegetable helped me, but I remember that I fasted. Cystitis, when fasting, unleashes all its power and you may have to stay in bed, but it will last three or maximum four days before disappearing completely.

Treatment of pain and chronic fatigue (exhaustion)
The presence of faeces in the rectum can greatly increase the pain of cystitis (as well as many other diseases) and can cause even more severe heartburn, fatigue and exhaustion, as well as other problems. Therefore, check that your rectum is always clean, especially when you feel sick in any way, especially if it is severe or chronic. **The rectum is the control centre of**

pain in the human body for many diseases and for many different situations of pain. If it is clean, pain subsides as if by magic, if not, the pain may persist. I repeat, in my humble opinion, this is involved in many different diseases, and therefore should be checked several times a day. Forgive me and please don't be shocked, but to perform this check you do not need to push hard or use a clyster, just insert your middle finger, because in a sick person faeces stop in the rectum without his knowledge or without any stimulation to defecate. Some faeces may stick inside the rectum and may need some helping out with your finger. The relief is instantaneous. One particular hygienist taught me a lot (to whom I turned to do fasting) that proved to be very useful.

This cleaning action, in my opinion, should be known by all those who suffer.

Eliminate: coffee, rice and all dairy products. Eat little, some aubergine, fish, pasta or buckwheat. Avoid too much salt and fried food.

Diabetes: buckwheat instead of bread and pasta.

In infections of any kind in any organ, use the same concept of eliminating foods, especially dairy products, eggs, too much meat, foods containing yeast, frozen vegetables and sweets with colourings and chemicals. And eat very little.

Also for some rare diseases, such as cystic fibrosis, all the above concepts apply: no dairy products. Change cereal and stick to buckwheat.

Do not be scared by the name of the disease, change your diet and if you still suffer, seriously consider semi-fasting.

Before an operation, for any reason, consider a few days of semi-fasting!

Anal fissures

I know someone who, not wanting to change diet or fast, cured anal fissures with a small enema of chamomile infusion once a day for ten days. He had constipation and consequently the fissures hurt him even more. He had tried everything, no end of ointments, even a cream pushed on him by his general practitioner for the modest sum of 90 Euros for a 20g tube, which brought absolutely no results.

To reduce swelling in a limb, the belly or very swollen intestines:
1) Quit smoking (for whoever smokes)
2) Eat fish, even canned tuna
3) CHAMOMILE infusion in the evening without sugar
Cigarettes: Avoid smoking especially immediately after eating rice.
4) Cooked cauliflower.

To Lose Weight: Eat mainly rice, with cooked courgettes, radicchio, fresh tomatoes or raw cabbage.
Alternate rice with pasta.
Avoid: other cooked vegetables, eggs, too much meat, too much cereal, wholegrain cereals, puffed rice.
Do not smoke, drink less coffee.
Eat fish, even canned tuna.
For those who are very weak and debilitated:
Grated carrot, cooked cabbage.
Aubergine with pasta.
Rice or pasta with radicchio.
Rice with boiled fish.
Fruit during the day as a snack.

For renal colic: I do not have direct experience with this, but my mother, who is now 73 years old, has suffered from renal colic for a lifetime, with frequent renal gravel in urine tests. One day a few years ago, I suggested to her to stop eating too much cooked vegetable, as she always ate every day boiled aubergine or boiled courgettes, or courgettes, peppers and aubergine all together.
She stopped cooking and eating all those vegetables and ever since she has no longer suffered from renal colic.

For mood disorders and mental illnesses:
Avoid especially rice and dairy products.
Stop smoking.
Cabbage with pasta.
Or aubergine with buckwheat
Boiled potato with salad.
Buckwheat with turnip.
Cooked tomato is the anti-depression fruit!
Semi-fasting and fasting.

For the liver and the sight:
The same as I have already said above, a cooked vegetable and a cereal. Spinach and pasta are the most suitable. Radicchio and boiled fish. A herbal tea of Artemisia, or mugwart, to help expel gallstones, with just one teaspoon of mugwort in a cup of water boiled for five minutes and drunk ten minutes after lunch. **For those who have swollen capillaries in the eye (trachoma), avoid legumes and especially beans.** Great for sight is buckwheat and fish, and pasta and spinach.

After vomiting, and for the swelling of the stomach and intestines: beans, avocado.

Important: in periods of healing, always eat Yin (cooked vegetables or fish) before and Yang (cereals) after. Wait 5 to 10 minutes between the 2 foods. For example, eat spinach first, wait 10 minutes and then eat pasta. This is because the spinach, which are Yin, works by cleaning and opening up the body, and the pasta, which is Yang, ends the process, bringing the content downwards in the body.
The most effective food cure that I know requires you to eat only 2 foods at each meal, without anything else. Only allowing time for the curative foods to act, without introducing other foods, you will soon get results. Our guts are full of bacteria and they cause almost all diseases. **The Natural Diet proposed here allows our body to feed, but does not give nourishment to the harmful bacteria, which return to the gut to be safely evacuated.**

This is how we heal. It is clear that you will feel a little hunger (or simple mental desire), but it is crucial to know how to control yourself, for at least 10-15 days. When you begin to feel a strong sense of hunger, you must resist it for at least another 2-3 days, to consolidate and improve the resulting healing.

Dieting, for example, on only spinach and pasta accelerates the healing process, which is accomplished in the days you feel greater hunger.

Bones, teeth and nails: grated carrots, aubergine.

Eyes (myopia): spinach and pasta, spinach and buckwheat, fish and buckwheat.

Neuralgia: no fried potatoes, rice or meat. Ok are desserts, fish, buckwheat.

Teeth: aubergine, fish, grated carrot, pasta. No dairy products.

Intestine: no dairy products or meat, no raw vegetables (except carrots).

Intestinal cramps: no meat, rice or raw carrots. Ok is fish, pasta, buckwheat, green cabbage, cooked cabbage and buckwheat instead of usual cereals.

Otitis: no dairy products, meat, rice or too much cereal. Ok is aubergine and buckwheat, and fish. Little fruit. Green cabbage or cooked cabbage.

Boiled potatoes and pasta, another valid combination for toothache.

I have been able to test the effect of non-filtered and natural (i.e. not in sachets) chamomile infusions. I drank them after dinner (better to skip dinner altogether or eat really little), with two tablespoons of chamomile in a glass of water and no sugar added, and here's what happened to me: in two days I healed a fractured finger that had been aching for months, despite my diet of fish, fruit, vegetables and cereals, and I felt considerable relief from bloating and many other problems of the intestine and body. **Chamomile greatly increases the number of white blood cells**. So chamomile is good for bones, teeth and intestines.

Who eats too much and all in one meal, with an appetizer, first course, second course, cheese, vegetables and coffee, will never notice which foods are good for him and which harm him. In such a mix of foods you cannot distinguish the day after what was positive and what was not. Only a bipolar diet, with only two elements at each meal, allows its practitioners to understand which foods to choose, day by day.

This diet is the most delicate, digestible and safe there is in nature. It is recommended for those who suffer from any illness or who are very delicate, even for very young children.

Cook everything with just a little water, a little olive oil and a little salt. Have only two main meals a day.

Once cured, you can begin again to eat almost everything!

Which illnesses can be cured in this simple way, you can discover with your own experience. Those who suffer can easily adjust their diet as I did. My experience of this diet is that I no longer take any medicine, having managed to cure various diseases that I had borne ever since I was a child. And now I have finally stopped suffering.

I cured chronic diseases of decades, chronic and antibiotic-resistant infections, tooth decay and toothache (I lost many teeth over the years because of my poor health and chronic diarrhoea) and I amazingly recovered my sight. I want to make clear that the healing takes place during two weeks of dietary cure and is consolidated by continuing.

Food, if eaten in small measure and well-chosen, is, for me, a powerful and unique medicine that God the Creator has provided for humanity, if we know how to use it.

The many medical tests that I was subjected to over the course of years, particularly colonoscopy (three very painful times), but also vaccinations for allergies, thermal water nasal flushes for antibiotic-resistant otitis and so on, served absolutely no purpose in curing me.

IMPORTANT NEWS

Watch on the website of Italia 1, on the programme "Le Iene", the educational history of a man **cured of an already metastasized brain cancer with a vegetarian diet**. Episode of 5th March, 2014:

http://www.video.mediaset.it/video/iene/full/443507/puntata-del-5-marzo.html

About a drug that can kill but is still sold in Italy:
http://www.lafucina.it/2014/03/14/il-farmaco-che-puo-uccidere-ma-che-in-italia-e-venduto/#

On a website about Swedish research. Topic: the development of antibiotic resistance, few hopes and little optimism:
http://www.forskning.se/nyheterfakta/teman/antibioticresistance/tenquestionsandanswers/isitpossibletostopthedevelopmentofresistance.5.1fcdf482138244d18752de.html#.UzF6N6RqAjg.facebook

From the newspaper website 'Il Sole 24 ORE.com'. Pity that there is no date, but it should be from 2012! Years of silence and misinformation!
http://salute24.ilsole24ore.com/articles/14643-guarisce-dal-cancro-al-colon-cambiando-dieta-frutta-e-verdura-lo-salvano

There isn't just clear mistreatment in the public health system, there is also a subtle violence of daily intimidation, more or less veiled threats and provocations, all to the detriment of the sick. And woe betide if you refuse to take those drugs, which make you feel terrible, they'll only give you even more. And with FORCE:
http://genova.repubblica.it/cronaca/2014/04/11/news/savona_violenze_su_malati_psichiatrici_dodiciarresti_per_maltrattamenti-83294065/

My education in natural cures developed by attending several fasting therapy and vegan nutrition centres. It was there, in 1999 or so, that I came to learn that many people in hygienist centres were being cured of the most severe and various diseases by semi-fasting.

I have to point out, though, that I personally distanced myself from these schools of thought on natural medicine because I found them too extremist. Eating only fruit (for months or years, as I have seen it practiced by some hygienists) seemed to lead to great physical and psychological problems, loss of teeth, excessive weight loss and loss of ability to concentrate.

I was not convinced by the raw food diet either. Too much water in the stomach brings the difficulty of keeping it. Then, I do not believe that those disgusting blended vegetable juices for days on end are necessary to cure oneself. And it is extremely difficult to stick to the plan. For people like me who have had severe intestinal problems such as diarrhoea it is certainly not recommended to eat principally raw vegetables, which clearly inflate the stomach and aggravate diarrhoea. There are, to my knowledge, no raw plant foods (except apples) that inhibit diarrhoea, while cooked cabbage works extremely well.

Also, a diet of mainly raw food, more seriously, leads to the decalcification of teeth and many other problems. Raw foodists that I know personally are all very thin and weak. Man is not a goat; plant food is fine, but mostly cooked, or otherwise balanced between raw and cooked! And results are achievable without eating only raw foods, in no time at all, just by eating little. This is much more important than eating only raw vegetables, which is, after all, unnatural and does not allow you to enjoy a good and healthy cuisine.

The Macrobiotics which proposes eating only rice for ten days was in my eyes another absurdity, and too dangerous for the mind and body. After years of trying, some research and a little fasting, I finally found the right way, which lies precisely in eating only two foods at each meal, mainly cooked and limited in quantity, as I have described above.

This, perhaps, is the synthesis of the many writings and many naturist schools, but it is an easy way that leads to great satisfaction over time. The other schools of dieting and natural cures offer only ways that are tough to follow, hard to practice and to maintain over time.

Finally, I believe that my system of dieting could also be helpful for our animal friends when they are sick: cooked cabbage and cereal, rice, pasta, buckwheat and fish! What food do dogs with dental problems normally receive from their masters?

Spread the word of this content, talk to your friends, make it known to the elderly, the sick, the suffering and children. Try it out and learn, change the world, really help those who suffer. Drugs, chemical medicines and antibiotics are almost all extremely harmful and do not heal anyone.

This information is the result of years of study and personal trials, research that I carried out in complete independence dictated only by the necessity provoked by my suffering. As someone who was once extremely sick of many ills, I wonder: how come there are people being cured with alternative natural methods to modern medicine, but still there is a silence on it all? How come those eminent doctors do not do their utmost to publicize these facts? How come people recover spontaneously without medicine? Because they VOLUNTARILY and UNKNOWINGLY change their diets, maintaining the change for several days, acting on instinct. This is how I cured even my teeth! Teeth are but one part of our body and I am convinced that even teeth can be cured with the right diet (mainly eliminating dairy products!).

Here below is, however, one effort by physicians: a city billboard, which tells the minimum (but essential) truth about antibiotics. And is this all they have to say about the ineffectiveness of medical care? Shouldn't there be more said?

Without rules antibiotics have no effect. Always follow your doctor's instructions. Do not take antibiotics to treat colds or flu infections. "This cartel was published by AIFA: Italian Drug Agency".

While it is true that a person with allergies has a higher sensitivity to allergens, pollen, dust, mould etc., in my experience, allergies and even asthma are certainly not cured by taking antihistamines, but wholly disappear after elimination of certain foods, something that no doctor ever I advised me to do.
And as for asthma and allergies, so it is true for all the other illnesses that I have mentioned. Medicines are for me only palliative, with so many serious side effects. Only natural dieting gave me to true healing.

The effects of the "care" of public psychiatrists.
Here are just some of the HARMFUL EFFECTS I suffered from 2001 to 2013 inclusive.

1) Sleeping fifteen hours a day, for several years.
2) Weight gain from 68 kg up to 105 kg in less than a year. Throughout my life, I had always been thin and I never went over 67-68 kg!
3) Diarrhoea fifteen times a day, for years, something almost unbelievable. I would get up in the morning and then have to run constantly between toilet and bed until about one o'clock in the afternoon, with a resulting state of exhaustion and intolerable pain.
4) No sexual activity.
5) Memory loss.
6) Total loss of physical strength.
7) Impossibility to work.
8) Inability to breath as soon as I went to bed and sleep apnoea that would wake me up suddenly in a state of total panic.
9) Feeling constantly sick, for months and years.
10) Drug-induced hallucinations!
11) Drug-induced fears (Zi … xa primarily, but also others)
12) Severe damage to teeth.
13) Much more.

Zi ... xa and many other psychoactive drugs reduced me to this state.

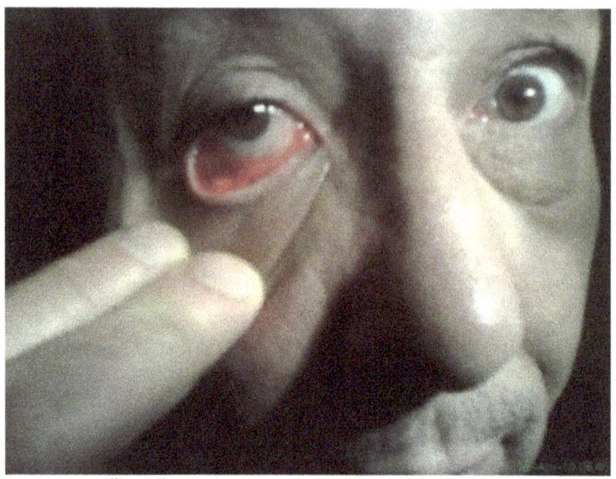

The effects of the psychiatric "cures" they forced on me.

After the fasting of 2009.

Sorry, but getting sick in Italy of mood and behavioural disorders could happen to anyone, but does receiving these and other **"services"** seem normal?

My name is Riccardo Tomasi. I was born in Trieste, but I live in Brescia. I am 51 years old. I attended a Classical Lyceum and I graduated with 46/60. I attended university but was not able to graduate.

My father is a retired senior officer of the Italian Air Force and Knight of the Italian Republic.

My grandfather Nereo, from Friuli, was a professor of mathematics and the cello. He was much loved by his students to whom he gave evening in accounting for free during the Second World War. He was also a world-class chess player and taught me the game when I was 3 years old. He died prematurely of hepatitis at 64, leaving my dear grandmother Amelia alone for the next 40 years.

My dear great-grandfather Antonio, father of Nereo, was a decorated colonel of the Italian Army, having fought in World War I. Then he worked in the dry ice industry.

Grandpa George, an industrialist, from Trieste born and breed, was simply an extremely nice person.

Go World little book: you can bring true healing to all those who suffer.

Bibliography

Manuel Lezaeta, "Natural Medicine Available to All".
Georges Ohsawa, "The Macrobiotic Diet".
Georges Ohsawa, "Natural Cures for Incurable Disease".
Herbert Shelton, various books on fasting.
Jean Valnet, "Heal Yourself With Vegetables, Fruits & Grains".

Thank you to the publisher www.youcanprint.it of Lecce, Italy, for the kindness and professionalism of their team.

Printed in the month of August 2015
on behalf of Youcanprint Self - Publishing